What Jobs Do They Do?

by Jimena Reyes

NATIONAL
GEOGRAPHIC
L E A R N I N G

T0349321

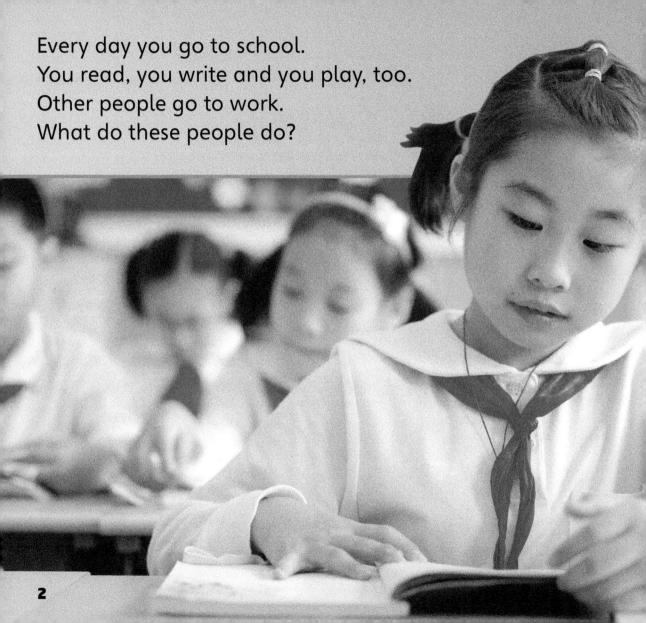

Every day you go to school.
You read, you write and you play, too.
Other people go to work.
What do these people do?

This person works with pets.
She works with quite a few.
She always helps sick animals.
What does this person do?

3

This woman is a vet!

She takes care of cats and dogs.
She even helps sick birds and goats,
and horses, sheep and frogs!

vet

This person works at a cooker.
He makes good food for you.
This person uses pots and pans.
What does this person do?

This man is a chef!

You can see him in his kitchen.
He is cooking pizza, fish and eggs,
and soup with rice and chicken.

chef

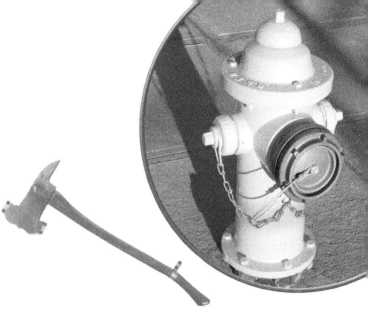

This person wears a special hat.
His coat is special, too.
He goes to work in an engine.
What does this person do?

This man is a firefighter!
He's ready all day long
to fight fires and help people.
He's very big and strong.

firefighter

8

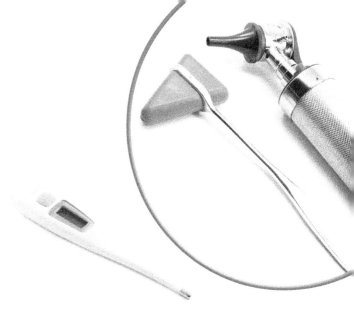

When you are feeling ill,
this person takes care of you.
She's often at a hospital.
What does this person do?

This woman is a doctor!
She listens to your heart.
Nurses often help her.
She's really very clever.

doctor

There are so many different jobs.
These jobs are just a few.
Some day when you grow up,
what do you want to do?

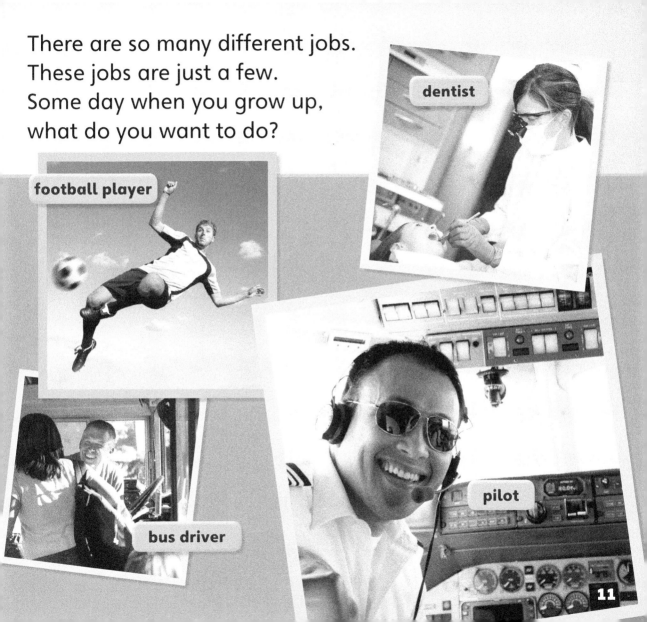

dentist

football player

bus driver

pilot

Facts About Dog Workers

Did you know that some animals have jobs, too? They are not bus drivers, dentists or pilots. But they do work. Here are some jobs that dogs do.

Some dogs help people in danger.

Some dogs work with other animals.

Some dogs help people who cannot see.

Some dogs are even film stars!

Some dogs pull sledges across the snow.

Fun with Jobs

Draw a line to match.

chef

bus driver

firefighter

doctor

vet

Write the name of each worker.

nurse   pilot   chef   film star

1. _____pilot_____

2. _____

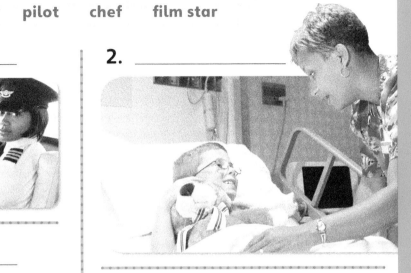

3. _____

4. _____

Glossary

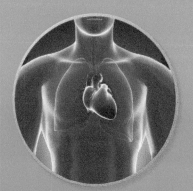

heart

hospital

pans

pets

pots

ill